Also by Gita Ralleigh

A Terrible Thing   (Bad Betty, 2020)

SIREN

Gita Ralleigh

ISBN: 978-1-915079-69-5

Cover designed by Aaron Kent

Edited and typeset by Aaron Kent

Broken Sleep Books Ltd
Rhydwen,
Talgarreg,
SA44 4HB
Wales

Contents

One of the mythical monsters, half-woman and half-bird, said by Greek poets to entice seamen by the sweetness of their song to such a degree that the listeners forgot all and died of hunger. The word thus came to be applied to any alluring woman.

— *Brewer's Dictionary of Phrase and Fable*

In Homer, the Sirens are winged creatures: the Muses clipped them for their failure. By the Renaissance, their feathers have switched for a mermaid's scaly tail.

— Sarah Howe, *Loop of Jade*

Siren

Gita Ralleigh

For Rohan and Leela

Mermaid Visits the Archive

After Adrienne Rich

By the shore, she recalls
once diving the wreck.

Though they told her never
to adventure its depths

or harvest its bones, cast
as oracle on ocean floor.

She witnessed a rotten hull
give way, from tarry gloom

the dull gleam of mercury,
copper ingots' cold clink.

She longs to recall the stink
of death. No documents

but papered dissolution.
She seeks herself in ivory

and iron, salt-cured skins,
elephant tusks, stone shot,

fragments of pelvis. Later
she learns to hide her tail

beneath long skirts. Land–
dweller, she gathers a form

from museum dust. Between
mammoth & meteorite, she

reads of affinity with elephants,
her twin pairs of breasts—how

when strapped to a mast, she
gains ecstasies—a voice pitched

to scream, which some sailors
call her song. She feels the stones

weighting her chest. Ghosts of
coins spill silver from her mouth.

the sea knows no borders

mermaid thinks dredged from
green depths of sorrow asked how
she did not drown like the others
who are her people   flag   nation
his land dweller teeth
predatory as shark fin
his gaze shoals her breasts
              her mercuric tail
she bares fierce pointed dentition
remains swan mute
until he grasps her matted hair
underneath
the red gape
   clavicle to nape
                  of narrow neck
wonderstruck
he explores the wound
      prises its silent mouth open
pain emerges
a cetacean keening   for the dead

Mermaid Becomes Merwife

Hands slashed by coral and rock,
flowering stems bleed on her palms.

Swaddled in silk to conceal her tail:
six woven yards of crimson brocade.

Wedding guests in scarlet or saffron—
blue or green risk summoning oceans.

A woman paints eyes on closed lids,
another plaits gold in sea tangle hair.

Wrists bound to his, mermaid feels
the sacred fire tongue at her throat.

Softly, a priest chants incantations.
He yanks her chain until she nods *yes*.

Merwife Dreams of the Circus

A fairground rush, the calliope's
　　　　clamour. No more
forsaken shores—she wants screams,
　　　　easy thrills. Painted, pinned

as careless knives whirr & slick
　　　　past, she'll backbend,
waterfall hair, balance glasses
　　　　on a belly laced in scars.

Breasts spangled, she'll sling trapeze
　　　　with delphine grace, whip the
crowd to a roar. Round up sealions,
　　　　make them bark in tune.

Bareback rider, circling the ring,
　　　　she'll side-saddle midnight
until her finale of fire, gulped down
　　　　like seawater or gin.

Later, she'll scrub at wax skin, dab
　　　　kohl eyes & coral lips, brace
her whalebone hips. Flop on a stoop,
　　　　smoke driftwood sticks.

At first light, she'll unbrick the wheels,
　　　　bid so long to yesterday. Roll on
tomorrow, always a new city, tiny
　　　　lights pricking the horizon.

Merwife Abandons the Suburbs

The day she leaves home, every car alarm on the street rings with siren simultaneity. What are they telling her? Only water knows, moving within her body: an oceanic feeling of intuition or warning. She walks to the bus stop past kids calling and shoving in a confusion of hormones. *We've explored just 5% of the ocean floor* says a girl. *There's 95% we know nothing about.* The winter sky is clear and sharp as inhalation. A pale yellow slant of shoreline. Once she shucked her armour to assimilate. Now she prepares to harden, turn calloused, chitinous. It hurts at first, but the water is icily numbing. Anaesthetic. Her skin scrapes rocky shallows, her soles, ribboned by shards, branch coral fronds of blood. She drifts deeper, stones cupped in each clenched fist freight her down. Scales glint forth, tiny slivers of teeth seam both her calves. Silvering is an adaptation, a camouflage, mirroring the sea's luminosity. Soon, she'll become invisible.

on the female monster

i

the monster's body is a cultural hybrid
defying annexation
with green vapour
& polyphony
vitality stalks
her imperilled hair
both warning & portent
she wreaks desire &
feminine upheaval

ii

the monster always escapes
with her freakish propensity
to shift and vanish like bones
or geographic talisman
she fragments aberration
with a dangerous refusal
bifurcating
and/or
either/or

iii

the monster is the harbinger
we are violated
in the cyber resistance
of the monster's body
which logically devours
hypermasculine &
divisive human
history

iv

the monster dwells at the gates
the undead ocean
returns to live among us
a dispossessed hydra
the planet in pain
incorporated
as haunting

v

the monster polices the borders
of grotesque prohibition
two living bodies
engulfed & bound
she & them
virago! lilith! sycorax!

vi

fear of the monster is really desire
every sublime glimpse
cast as sculpted dance
lascivious imaginary
exoticised beauty
disturbing rape

vii

the monster stands at the threshold
asks us how
asks us why
asks us what
is sanctioned
what is forbidden

Most people come in these days asking

for the robot.
Her accumulated wisdom, fed
by crimson delicacy. Plump dexterity
of four metal arms, her civilian sensors,
implants and fishhooks at your breast.
Enhancing, mimicking, performing genie
she emerges theatrical in smoke plumes
latent with connectivity, buffering sweet
manoeuvrability to open hearts.
Glimpse amazement as five hundred
magnified mesmeric faces suggest
permanently palpable human friend.
No guesswork. Her intuitive intimacy
machine deftly probes much deep, dark,
sexual hurting.
With dedicated incisions, she pincers all
critical traces of *end of the last century* trouble.
Wince and wonder. She is both diagnosis & cure.

Dreaming Blue

You close your eyes to an oneiric hum of darkness.
Feel the water's insistence, how calm latency stirs.

Symbols arise, slow birthed from refractive deep.
Minor tentacled creatures surface, writhe amid

a milk froth of waves. Always alone in dreams, you
comb littorals on broken mnemonic shorelines.

Saltwater corrodes silence. When you speak in old,
eroded tongues, it's too late. The sea will not sing its

ancient history, nor jettison epiphany to you: struck
mute, no song worth sharing. Refusals are wracked at

your mouth's open cave. Wiping grit from your eyes,
you watch whales on the remote horizon, sounding in

monumental curved skulls. Imagine blue-skinned Vishnu,
adrift on Ananta, the serpent. When the world becomes

hopelessly oceanic and playful, Vishnu begins to dream
of a golden lotus seeding his navel. How on its blooming

a cosmos scatters. Once more, the universe spins.

sedna song

i am a thin crack in new ice
a low race of moon-tides
    ivory comb of bone
name my creatures   seal   blackfish whale

the birdman
pecks breasts   claws my hair
swoops eyes   gouges at scalp
immense   thrashing
wings   stun

birdman   will not
have me   leave him

mirror   shatters
over   black head
his kayak   scuds grey waters
sea-bird cry   rakes white skies
i sink   into green
glass   depths

name my creatures   seal   blackfish whale
    ivory comb of bone

a low race of moon-tides
i am a thin crack in new ice

to become an island

       of your own self woman   let waves
break hard upon your rocks   let lone sailors fleeing
squalls navigate your edges

       allow only drowning men   adrift & castaway
to find your shores   let them thirst for your fruit
yearn to keep you in thrall.

       curse them to earn it   to lose compass
& cargo to crawl   burning sands naked   seek
your oasis in a salt desert

       if you choose   shake clouds from hair
ease storms by hand   lull hippocampi to sleep   dream
honeyed chant of uncharted deep

Satyavati

If you close your eyes to dream, do you hear the wind caress trees?
Or a tumult of spuming river, the oar's blade cutting water's skin.

And swift metal shoals of arrows. Death, a slew of moonlit fish
to gaped shark mouth. *Every living thing is always dying,* our Delphic

mother sang, her pallor blue as the skies. She told us her curse:
to split and birth us earth-tinged twins. We set her free of course.

Metamorphic apsara, winging away from a riverine past, she left
my brother and I half-drowned. The fisher-folk crowned him

king of the river, while I, Matsyagandha, ammoniacal fish girl, was
shamed for spawning dynasties that came bringing devastation.

All because the man who took me called himself holy. Old wolf.
Forced me onto the island, conjured up darkness black as kajal.

He cleansed my fish stink, anointed me with fragrant purity,
stripped my innocence and restored it. Magic. All of it horseshit.

Technically, it was a virgin birth. My son passed into immortality,
authored the book you're reading to tell you: they're all the same.

Gods, holy men, kings. Slack-jawed, lusting for the stench of power.

Heirlooms

This long black plait
coiled in a drawer
once it whipped at her ankles.
Her wedding sari
burnt orange brocade
woven from purest
zari thread.
A sitar, strung for each
of twenty-one years.
Mahogany curves recline,
never played.
Many years since a bride
with no dowry
left home forever,
severed the spill
of hair inking dirt
as she flung her
head to laugh.
Fresh pip of light
within her, my birth
unintended.
A half formed, not
wanted thing–
I didn't mean to hear
her testament: strings
lamenting sympathy,
a tarnished gold

gleam of mandarin silk.
Sandalwood breath
from her rope
of dead hair.

Small Gods

For Rani Gaidinliu

At seven, I asked mother for paper
to write. My hand swept in circles.
Within the cave's inked dark, I read
inscriptions, lit gold by divine aura.

To write, my hand swept in circles.
Lines flickered, dimmed in stone—
inscriptions lit with an aura. Only I
divined their golden spiral of thread.

Lines flickered alive and dimmed:
I traced the runes in bull's blood,
recoiled at the long red thread
of a python's forked tongue.

I wrote symbols in bull's blood.
My cousin declared small gods dead,
by a python's forked tongue. Only an
indigo sky god was fit for worship.

Now the small gods were dead,
in a notebook, my hand's script
named the sky god fit for worship.
North, South, East, West, unfolded

from a notebook, lettered in my hand.
My land of sacred mountains. People
North, South, East, West, unfolding
wide as a map of woven cloth. Mine,

this land of holy mountains. People
damned me as sorceress. Called me
queen of a scrap of woven cloth. My
youth locked away from my body,

damned as a sorceress, called queen,
I begged my jailers for paper and ink.
My youth burned out like a candle.
Eyes half-shut, I dreamed of the cave.

Trilogy

I

Opening shot. *Girl* on a battlefield. The camera pans numberless dead. Round black mouths slack open, defeated fish gulp a copper-tinged sky. They lie cadaverous, shaven-headed, eye-patched, skin-sutured. Close-up, *Girl* is unblemished: hair pure & whip-like or chestnut & tumbling. Pale eyes of steel grey or verdigris. Her armour welded from hubcaps & tyre, tailored skin-tight, hip-hugged by slick holsters. Slung upon her lithe spine a quiver of arrows. Arching her back, she squints, takes aim like Gramma showed her. Gramma died of the end times like everyone *Girl* loved. *Girl* is alone now. Two actors vie for her affections: one a music star the other an influencer, to represent old & newly dystopian worlds.

II

Girl embodies apocalyptic renewal: cityscape of exhausted rubble, farms burned stubble. Techne mere fire, spit & old wire powered by batteries from innards of infernal machines. See *Girl* parkour cyborg precision over rusted hills, burnished gold sky, mercurised river. Embittered, embattled *Girl* meets her rival's gaze down a gun barrel. Weeps only when she loses the bronze talisman about her neck. A dragonfly wing? (No. It is literally a seed pod.)

III

So many years of her life pass for six hours of film. At trilogy's fin, *Girl* walks lone charnel ground. Dodges bullet rain, seeps fake blood to fill a river. She's tired of the influencer, whom she wants to kill. The music star is secretly married. Ending a wintertime of spare & barren, we are reminded *Girl* will flourish. *Girl* will blossom in spring, bear fruit at fall. Epilogue of fields tinted saffron. Grass, wildflower, corn & hayseed. Settler recuperation. A land left unclaimed (like a woman) is no nation. *Girl* in floral frock holds baby: cute assembly of violence & desire, celebrity & guilt without reparation. **Fadeout.**

Haunted

For Amrita Sher-Gil

Grey dawn over Paris cobblestones,
Gauloises winter wreathed blue in smoke.
Electric streetlight lent faces a yellow patina,
your body an essay in exoticism. Rained upon,
lovers taken, you licked powdered sugar
off each red fingertip. Why were you here?
Your forsaken shadow—where did it hide?

An ocean away, home unsheathed its claws.
India belongs only to me, you whispered.
Desire in darkness, lit by guttering lamp wicks.
Clay-pot water spilled on the necks of young girls.
Bit chilli stung your ghee-dipped tongue. You
licked mango nectar, rivulets between thighs.
Stone of the fruit lodged deep in the body.

Your shadow rose, a lush spectre. Betrayal arrayed
upon a pyre's soot flame. *Perhaps it will fly away.*

Tending the Epiphyte

               Like the banyan

I blew here   seeded windswept   on unwilling host.

Here I branched   took root among strangers.

As strangler fig

      I put out shoots

           strained for the light   my

               radicles sought hard soil.

I rose   branching in multiplicity   readied for fight.

Tried to recall lost

          songs of bulbul

     cries of mynah

calls of koel.

Summon an understory of memory:

      interiors sugared in molasses

         hissed steam   off cotton saris

           slap   of naked feet

               tongue-burn   fresh roti.

How much of this   is invention   entanglement   complicity?

How to unbind

     this mesh

       of surging roots?

        Allow the wasps to swarm

           tender fruit   resin gall in amber.

   Tend to the epiphyte

          ignore the hollow core.

      Leave it to devour

    its own empty flesh   scented rind.

ghazal: *manohara*

i heard flight was three parts belief, a body three parts water. wait—
you called me half-bird. my habitus gravity: ornamentally winged.

fleshed breast, thigh, marrow-boned carmine, lacunae of air sate
with blood. watch them tremble, invisible, my stilled wings.

you looped my foot to trip me, knew i'd plummet. it will take
so long to rid me of man-stink, of this noose, circled like a ring.

since your barb pierced tender skin, let hunter's snare break
loose—i'll worry the knot embracing my ankle, claw at the strings.

when I forsake you, consider me elemental. my brow's arch fate
sacrificed to you, lover—didn't you place this ring on my finger?

weighted terrestrial by terror, not joy, watch me arrow escape,
see it fly—how my shadow swoops moons, near celestial being.

i'll soar to dominions of bark, sap, blossom—leave in my wake
those shackled days and nights. from holy mountaintop, i'll sing.

migrant mother sings as bird of myth

no more the bulbul
tethered to master's finger

red thread looped over a claw
longing for her faithless rose

grown tired of the ghazal

i have flown the poet's garden

the hoopoe is wise
she will tell your fate

give her a drop of blood

i bled for you

now tell me mine

consider the chataka
her beak widens ecstatic

she drinks falling raindrops
to heavensweet tears

this crest on my head

is a tight strung bow

or the chakor, her love
who wouldn't dream

for the moon is legend
nights lit by moonbeams

how they mercury

the blackest waters

saraswati rides the hamsa

a bird that feeds on pearls

i grind my teeth

turn pearls into dust

the hamsa is held sacred
flies through air

she walks earth
swims in water

as i have walked on water swum air

flown face down in dirt

the huma bird soars so high

her eggs hatch on the wing

helpless

    fledglings   gasp

          tumbled   air

mastering flight

    moments before

    hitting

            hard ground

my shadow passes over each fallen one   *anoints them kings*

How women   *become*   *birds*

Achelous' daughters	transformed to Sirens	for love
Alcyone	transformed to a kingfisher	for love
Meleager's sisters	transformed to guinea hens	for grief
Nyctimene	transformed to an owl	for incest
Scylla	transformed to a rock dove	for betrayal
Arne	transformed to a jackdaw	for betrayal
Procne	transformed to a swallow	for revenge
Philomela	transformed to a nightingale	for revenge
Anius' daughters	transformed to doves	**for escape**
Coronis	transformed to a crow	**for escape**
Combe	transformed to a bird	**for escape**

Crow's True Song

In the early glint of sun, she caws me awake
from the mango tree. Old scrapethroat rakes
trembling air, shirrs green leaves and a stupor
of sucking bees. She will not quiet her raucous
creak, nor still curved beak for other's trilling.
Swooping to a mirror, she preens her nightglister
wings. Pecks her image in glass: kiss or sinister
shadow embrace? Her cry puckers my heart
to a scar—an ugly cry but true—this song
of crow, who loves herself. Why can't you?

song for lilith

if a woman walks alone   leaves behind her
pronged prints of taloned birds
they are not tracks   do not attempt pursuit
her zygodactyl feet indicate future   and past
dark maid of babylon   a loosed spirit
she fled   as the tree of life fell
her nightcry   usurped for a thief screech
you who fly in dark rooms, lilith be off, thief, breaker of bones

her airs devour   smallboned   entities
those that crawl   on the earth   unwinged
queen of the night   banished to wastes
she reigns in castles   overgrown by thorns
fortresses   thick with thistles and briars
here jackals rage   wildcats slink   satyrs cry
deep in nested shadows she lays her eggs
there shall the lilith repose, find herself a place to rest

unleash winds that twist howl moan
let wilderness   lay claim to the earth
o sister spirits   enlist the darkling light
ransack and storm   their noble cities
declare them forlorn
call all trees   once more the tree of life
as lilith once   was only adam's wife
now unbind the lilith from her chains

Auguries

When the birds were dead, we gathered
up their small and scattered heads. Fired
    them clean of charred flesh and feather,
scoured each to yellow dome. Bleached
    skulls lined long wooden tables like cups.
In leather aprons we took their measure:
    hollow of bone, lacunae of air, angle of bill,
gleam of eye. How breakable they seemed.

    Blasting them in floods of radiant atoms,
we summoned up life on whistle and pipe.
    Nothing. No song but quiet. Abandoned,
rows of hollow heads furred with dust.

    One by one they shattered; bones flinched
beneath our soles. We heard fluted notes,
    a sonation of winging ghosts brushed our eyes
as they rose. We were blameless. No lie. How
    should we know what futures the skulls of birds
foretold? Our ears too old to hear their singing.

Museum of Anatomy

Here's the task at hand. She will dissect, display the nerves
and muscle of the chest, blood vessels trembling reedy paths.
An airless room, braced with the stench of formalin. A jester
tosses the bones of the wrist: *scaphoid, capitate, lunate,* worn
as ivory dice. Around them are containers of dismantled bodies:
boxed, scrubbed skulls, glass-jars of perishable organs. First
she must lay scalpel to skin, flay it from delicate flesh, feel her
areoles shrink and darken in sensory response. At the anatomy
museum her mind wanders on improbable pathways. A *vanitas*
to consider one's own death. Does she want it science-fictional?
To end as brain in a jar, disembodied, soused in liquid selfhood.
Or magic realist: a darkly misshapen heart stuttering ionic love
from electrolyte bath. A poetic death, where bells ring only for
the pilgrim who has abandoned her empty temple. She hopes her
tongue is last to die: ululating small paroxysms of sound, of air

Ghazal: *Air*

Dark shell, white flesh, milk of coconut spills in the air.
We fly these ruins as birds, our losses wing the air.

Powder-white as the elephant an Emperor once sent.
Smoke rises from funeral pyres to sting the air.

Clothed in yellow silk, under rain of jasmine blooms.
Temple idols walk, their eloquent hands hymn the air.

Did we dream of fleeing our city as strangers?
Nephelomancy clouds danger, thunder djinns the air.

Their hunters steal sly victory, hack at gathered bones.
Our tiger skulls bullets: stripes blacken and skin the air.

We wander in labyrinths, gather songs in threadbare palms.
As a moth forsakes stars, we embrace flames, pin the air.

Notes

Mermaid Visits the Archive takes inspiration from *Diving into the Wreck* by Adrienne Rich and was anthologised in *Where We Find Ourselves* published by Arachne Press in 2021.

on the female monster uses found text from 'Monster Culture (Seven Theses)' by Jeffrey Jerome Cohen in *Monster Theory: Reading Culture* ed. Jeffrey Jerome Cohen, University of Minnesota Press 1996.

Most people come in these days asking appeared in *Tentacular* 2022. The poem uses found text (other than 'she' and 'her') from 'The robot will see you now: could computers take over medicine entirely?' Tim Adams, *The Guardian*, 2018.

Dreaming Blue Vishnu is the Hindu deity of creation. This poem refers to a myth from the Hindu Puranas, that the universe is created by Vishnu, dreaming.

sedna song Sedna is a sea goddess known by many different names in Inuit mythologies.

Satyavati In the *Mahabharata* Satyavati is the great-grandmother of both warring dynasties and also the mother of Vyasa, its author.

Heirlooms An earlier version of this poem was anthologised in *Hair Raising* published by Nine Pens press in 2021.

Small Gods Rani Gaidinliu, a leader of the Heraka movement in Northeast India, was imprisoned by the British at 16 and released on Independence, 15 years later. This poem is inspired by '"Lines that speak" The Gaidinliu notebooks as language, prophecy, and textuality' by Arkotong Longkumer, published in *Hau: Journal of Ethnographic Theory* 6 (2): 123–147, 2016.

Haunted takes inspiration from the life of painter Amrita Sher-Gil who had an Indian father and Hungarian mother and trained as a painter in Paris before returning to India.

Tending the Epiphyte first appeared in *harana poetry* in 2021.

ghazal: *manohara* Manohara in Buddhist mythology was a Kinnari, half woman-half bird, trapped by a hunter and married to Prince Sudhana.

***migrant mother sings* as bird of myth** The bulbul is the Indian nightingale. The chataka, chakor and huma are all birds of Indian mythology. The hamsa, a goose or swan, is the vahana, or vehicle of Saraswati, who is the Hindu goddess of music, learning and poetry.

how women become birds takes its transformations from Ovid's *Metamorphoses*.

Crow's True Song first appeared online in *Anthropocene* in 2020.

song for lilith Lilith was a demonic figure in Judaic mythology. This poem includes part of Isiah, verse 34.

Auguries first appeared in *Interpreter's House* in 2020.

Museum of Anatomy was first published in *Tentacular* in 2022.

Ghazal: *Air* was first published in *Poetry Birmingham* in 2022. After the siege of Seringapatam in 1799 in which Tipu Sultan, the ruler of Mysore, was killed, 300 women who lived in the Palace zenana (women's quarters) were transported two hundred miles to Madras.

Acknowledgements

Thank you to the editors of the journals and anthologies in which some of these poems first appeared, as well as the wonderful poets who saw (via The Poetry School) this work at an early stage: Khairani Barokka, Mona Arshi, Zakia Carpenter-Hall and Carrie Etter. Thanks also to the amazing Liz Berry, Tishani Doshi, Ranjit Hoskote, Vahni (Anthony Ezekiel) Capildeo, Shivanee Ramlochan, Rishi Dastidar and Nisha Ramayya for being sources of both inspiration and support.

As always, I'm eternally grateful to my dear sisters in the Kinara collective: Sarala Estruch, Anita Pati, Shash Trevett and Rushika Wick for their guiding light. And huge, huge thanks to the incredible Aaron Kent and the other beautiful souls at Broken Sleep, who give so much of themselves in order to help us lay out our unrest.

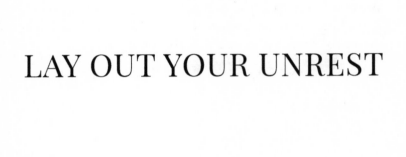

LAY OUT YOUR UNREST

Lightning Source UK Ltd.
Milton Keynes UK
UKHW041026080822
407000UK00003B/123